THE ASTROTWINS™ PRESENT

CAPRICORN

a cosmic roadmap to the stuff that matters

Published by Advance Publishers, L.C.
Maitland, FL 32751 USA
www.advancepublishers.com
Produced by Mediarology, Inc.
Designed by Mediarology, Inc.
© 2006 Advance Publishers, L.C.
Printed in the United States of America

ART & DESIGN
Creative Direction by Denise See
Illustrations by Bellinger Moye
For Mediarology, Inc.

SPECIAL THANKS
Dara Colwell, Amanda E. Edmund,
Trisha Malin, Adam Morgan

ABOUT THE AUTHORS
Identical twin sisters **Tali and Ophira Edut** (The AstroTwins™) are the authors of *Astrostyle: Star-studded Advice for Love, Life and Looking Good* (Simon & Schuster, 2003), and the astrologers for *Teen People,* HelloKitty.com and the Oxygen Network. Their horoscopes reach over 20 million readers a month. They've appeared on MTV's *TRL* and have dished astrological advice to the likes of Beyonce, Jessica Simpson and No Doubt. They've worked in publishing for over a decade, creating projects through their company Mediarology. Their past productions include *HUES,* an award-winning magazine for multicultural young women, and the book *Body Outlaws: Rewriting the Rules of Beauty & Body Image* (Seal Press, 2004). They live in New York City. Visit them online at www.astrostyle.com.

Capricorn

Dear Capricorn,

There's no mistake you were born under your sign! The moment you arrived was created just for you—and there will never be another one like it. Your astrological sign, which is determined by the date and time you were born, gifted you with unique talents, beauty, strength and challenges. Just as there are billions of stars in the sky, there's only one you in the universe. (As identical twins, we can attest to this!) So we're here to help you be your ultimate best, with the cosmos as your guide.

Let's face it: life isn't always easy. There will be tough times and obstacles to face. Life is full of questions: *Who's my best love match? How can I make more money, or find the job of my dreams? When should I get married, take a vacation, start a family, nurture my health?* Understanding yourself better makes it easier to answer those questions, and that's where the zodiac can help. So consider this book a roadmap to your soul, an operating manual for your life.

Truth is, you already have everything you need to live the life of your dreams. It's just about knowing what makes you shine, then polishing that diamond. So whether you're a princess cut or a solitaire, finding the perfect setting is the key to claiming the rich, fulfilling life that's your birthright!

Cosmic Love,
Ophira & Tali Edut
The AstroTwins

THE 12 ZODIAC SIGNS

Signs	Dates	Traits	Element
Aries	March 21–April 19	Passionate, daring, energetic	Fire
Taurus	April 20–May 20	Patient, stable, loyal, stubborn	Earth
Gemini	May 21–June 20	Adventurous, clever, scattered	Air
Cancer	June 21–July 22	Nurturing, intuitive, compassionate	Water
Leo	July 23–August 22	Dramatic, romantic, leaders	Fire
Virgo	August 23–September 22	Organized, helpful, critical	Earth
Libra	September 23–October 22	Charming, fair, indecisive	Air
Scorpio	October 23–November 21	Magnetic, intense, controlling	Water
Sagittarius	November 22–December 21	Inspiring, funny, tactless	Fire
Capricorn	December 22–January 19	Loyal, persistent, pessimistic	Earth
Aquarius	January 20–February 18	Original, unpredictable, rebellious	Air
Pisces	February 19–March 20	Dreamy, imaginative, secretive	Water

{All About}

Capricorn

Dates: December 22–January 19
Symbol: The Mountain Goat
Color: Gray
Ruling Planet: Saturn, the planet of ambition and discipline
Good Day: Loyal, patient
Bad Day: Depressed, stubborn
Favorite Things: Family reunions, history, trophies

04

Ambitious Capricorn is symbolized by a mountain goat climbing up a rocky hill, taking one cautious step at a time. And that's exactly how patient Caps like to do everything. You'll skip the good stuff today if it means getting the reward tomorrow. That's why your sign has more trophies and loyal friends than any other—you stay strong through the hard times. Hardworking Capricorns are devoted to their friends and families, and people count on you for support because you always keep your word. Remember to let yourself have fun, too! Life doesn't always have to be an uphill climb. It's okay to enjoy your victories, even if you didn't work hard to win them. Lighten up, loosen up, throw caution to the wind and share your wacky, down–to–earth humor. When you get moody, let your parents and closest friends be there for you—just as you always are for them.

Love, loyalty and sincerity are the hallmarks of your sign. Add sensitivity and sensibility to the mix, and Capricorn makes a disciplined romantic who's aiming for the perfect partner. You're a persistent soul who takes love seriously and is ready to stand by your significant other until the bitter end. Because flings aren't your bag, you may have already picked out your grandchildren's names by the second date, or you might end up marrying your high school sweetheart. Capricorn rules determination and long–term investments, which is exactly how you approach love. It must be worth the time and effort, or why bother?

As a status–conscious sign, you want a mate who makes you look good. It's not that you need a supermodel, just an ambitious, upstanding person you can take home to your parents. You're extremely loyal to your family and friends, so your partner must get along with them, or all bets are off.

Although you may appear ultra–serious, there's a wild woman waiting to be unleashed—at the appropriate time, of course. At times quiet and stoic, once you let down your guard, you can be loud and crude, with a wacky sense of humor. Your companions rely on you for your steady focus and earthbound perspective.

Turn–Ons: Respect and good values • Loyalty and security • Serious, ambitious people with impressive credentials • Someone who looks good on your arm

Turn–Offs: Love 'em and leave 'em types • A man without a plan • People who don't get along with your family and friends • Flighty, impractical people

Find Your Love Match!

Aries	Aries is the zodiac's baby, and Capricorn is the daddy. Serious Capricorn is amused by Aries' spunk. Aries feels grounded and secure with responsible Capricorn.
Taurus	Hello, loveliness. These two earth signs see eye–to–eye on so many issues. You're both practical and level-headed, with a taste for the finer things in life.
Gemini	Steady, patient Capricorn gives Gemini a stable foundation. Gemini lightens up serious Capricorn. If balanced right, you can harmonize and enjoy a strong attraction.
Cancer	Nurturing Cancer brings out serious Capricorn's sentimental side. Stable Capricorn holds it steady when Cancer's emotions run wild. You make a cozy combo.
Leo	You've both got first–class tastes and a wild streak. You look great in public together, and you love each other's power. Leo warms up cool Cap; Capricorn relaxes energetic Leo.
Virgo	You both want a stable, goal–oriented partner, and you find that in each other. Helpful Virgo nurtures hard-working Cap, while patient Capricorn relaxes Virgo.
Libra	Libra loves to be spoiled and babied; Capricorn happily brings home the bacon. Libra benefits from Capricorn's sound money management; serious Cap relaxes around lighthearted Libra.
Scorpio	You both love a challenge, and there are plenty of spicy power plays in this match. The intrigue and passion will keep you entertained. You also form a stable twosome.
Sagittarius	Sagittarius has the vision, and Capricorn supplies the follow–through. If you balance your differences, you form a strong and lasting bond.
Capricorn	You're both serious and traditional, with your eyes on a goal. You'll work loyally and tirelessly for any shared vision your create. If you commit, you're in it for the long haul.
Aquarius	You're both ambitious and a little eccentric. Earthy Capricorn stabilizes scattered Aquarius. The Aquarian playfulness can lighten Capricorn's heavy moods.
Pisces	Pisces brings the romantic fantasy world; Capricorn keeps one foot here on Earth. Your exciting plans will actually be fulfilled!

☠☠☠ = The stars are aligned!   ☠☠☠ = Simply divine

The Bad	*Rating*
Capricorn's practical style can crush Aries' playful spirit. Aries' explosive side upsets Capricorn's steady pace. You're both strong–willed and won't back down in a fight.	👹👹
Capricorn's simple tastes and lack of expressiveness may not satisfy Taurus's need for romance and luxury. You may both be too practical to keep the fires burning.	👹👹👹👹
Capricorn goes step by step and moves slowly. Gemini is a wild child who never stops moving. Unless you compromise, you won't be on the same page.	👹👹
Cancer's moodiness can send Capricorn fleeing for stability. Workaholic Capricorn may spend too much time on goals, leaving neglected Cancer without the loving' she needs.	👹👹👹
Capricorn is steady and reserved, while Leo is fast–paced and outgoing. Capricorn doesn't like to show emotions, but Leo needs to be openly adored. Your energy can clash.	👹👹
You bring out each other's stubborn, judgmental side. You both play it safe, but romance requires risk. Too much practicality could bore you.	👹👹👹👹
Trust alert! Libra's lightness could be interpreted as game–playing, and Capricorn is looking for a serious partner. If Capricorn adopts an all–work and no–play attitude, fun–loving Libra may look elsewhere.	👹👹
Power games are exciting until somebody gets hurt. You could leave each other feeling used and drained. Your intense ambition leaves little time for romance. Chill out!	👹👹👹
Sagittarius loves freedom and doing things her way. Capricorn is traditional and plays by the rules. Slow–moving Capricorn could frustrate impatient Sagittarius.	👹👹
Two workaholics in a relationship can kill the buzz. Who will lighten the mood and remind you to have fun? You may be too alike to keep the sparks flying.	👹
Capricorn is a rule–maker and Aquarius is a rule–breaker. Your values may clash. Capricorn's heaviness could also overwhelm lighthearted Aquarius, who just wants to have fun.	👹
Dreamy, rebellious Pisces annoys practical, rule–abiding Capricorn. Your shared moodiness could be a downer.	👹👹👹

👹👹 = Takes work to harmonize   👹 = A cosmic challenge

The Men
of the Zodiac

THE ARIES MAN (March 21–April 19)

THE WARRIOR | If you like a macho man who's not afraid to cry, the Aries man is for you! Ruled by energetic Mars, he wants to be your hero. As the zodiac's first sign, Mr. Aries can be a baby, and he needs plenty of attention. He'll test your patience, and he can be a tyrant if he doesn't get his way. As demanding as your Aries gets, he'll love you with equal intensity. The woman who gives him both security and freedom will win his heart.

Aries Men: Russell Crowe, Heath Ledger, Hugh Hefner, David Letterman, Jackie Chan, Vince Vaughn, Martin Lawrence, Alec Baldwin, Robert Downey Jr., Steven Tyler, Marlon Brando, Pharrell Williams

THE TAURUS MAN (April 20–May 20)

MR. FIREPLACE | Who's your daddy? The Taurus man may look like a playboy, but he's as stable as a suburban soccer dad. In fact, he's quite the family guy. Good–time girls looking for a fling need not apply. Sensual Taurus–boy plays for keeps, and he only wants the best. Don't rush him. He takes his time to make sure you're worth the investment. Once you're in, he'll treat you like a princess, pampering you with gourmet food and extravagant gifts. Be the total package and he's yours forever.

Taurus Men: Enrique Iglesias, Jack Nicholson, Tony Hawke, George Clooney, Jay Leno, Bono, Jet Li, Pierce Brosnan, Willie Nelson, Andre Agassi, Stevie Wonder, Billy Joel, Jerry Seinfeld, Tim McGraw, Jason Lee

Illustrations by Bellinger Moye

THE GEMINI MAN (May 21–June 20)

MR. ALL TALK & ALL ACTION | Attraction is in the mind for the Gemini man. He's adventurous, quirky and an original thinker. He needs mental and intellectual chemistry, and great communication. As the sign of the Twins, his personality is always changing, so you'll never be bored. However, stability doesn't come easy. The Gemini man can be hard to pin down, and he needs a strong woman who's not easily manipulated. Until he finally commits, he may drive you crazy with constant indecision. Once he comes around, though, he plays for keeps. Let the adventures begin!
Gemini Men: Johnny Depp, Donald Trump, Andre 3000, Lenny Kravitz, Prince, Colin Farrell, Michael J. Fox, Joshua Jackson, Morgan Freeman, Mike Myers, Dave Navarro, Kanye West, Mark Wahlberg, Tupac, Notorious B.I.G., Clint Eastwood

THE CANCER MAN (June 21–July 22)

THE ROMANTIC | The Cancer man is in touch with his "feminine side"—and proud of it! Even if he acts crabby or tough, there's a sensitive, intuitive heart beating under that manly chest. Cancer is a domestic sign, so this guy will keep the home fires burning. He's a family man, and has a strong relationship with his mother (be it good or bad). Sentimental and romantic, this loyal sign appreciates your femininity—curves and all. Like a crab, he can be insecure, and doesn't emerge from his shell until it's safe. Fickle types stay away! The Cancer man is possessive, even clingy, and doesn't take kindly to betrayal.
Cancer Men: Tom Cruise, Harrison Ford, Josh Hartnett, Prince William, John Cusack, 50 Cent, Bill Cosby, Beck, Tom Hanks, Jason Schwartzmann, George W. Bush, Will Ferrell, Mike Tyson, Robin Williams, Chris Cornell

THE LEO MAN (July 23–August 22)

MR. PASSION | The Leo man is a passionate romantic who wears his heart on his sleeve. Just adore him and he's yours. Depending on his maturity level, this guy is a knight in shining armor or an egomaniac. If you win a bold, sexy Leo man's heart, he'll shamelessly worship and spoil you. He wants the world to know you're his woman! He'll shower you with red roses and poetry, and he always wants to hold your hand. Busy types need not apply—the Leo man needs lots of attention. He's the king of the jungle. Could you be his queen?
Leo Men: Ben Affleck, Antonio Banderas, Bill Clinton, Robert Redford, Arnold Schwarzenaeger, Matthew Perry, Matt LeBlanc, Billy Bob Thornton, Mick Jagger, Woody Harrelson, Sean Penn, Daniel Radcliffe, Robert DeNiro

THE VIRGO MAN (August 23–September 22)

MR. CONVERSATION | You know that "diamond in the rough" who gets passed over for flashier types? Simple and understated, Mr. Virgo is the best–kept secret in town. He's just waiting for an intelligent, classy woman he can respect. The way to a Virgo's heart is through great conversation. He'll fall in love while analyzing a TV show, or debating why smoking should be banned. You'll fall for his baby face and the way he takes in every word you say.

Virgo Men: Marc Anthony, Hugh Grant, Sean Connery, Keanu Reeves, Charlie Sheen, Michael Jackson, Macaulay Culkin, Richard Gere, Jason Priestley, Ludacris, Ryan Phillippe, Benjamin McKenzie, David Arquette, Adam Sandler, Julian Casablancas, Dave Chappelle, Jack Black, Liam Gallagher, Lance Armstrong

THE LIBRA MAN (September 23–October 22)

THE THINKER | He's a cutie with dimples and perfect features, the guy who's not afraid to wear pastel shirts or watch a romantic comedy. The Libra man can't be rushed—he takes his time to commit—but once he's in, he's rock–steady. In fact, you may have to tip his scales to keep things exciting after a while. This guy loves beauty, and that goes for a beautiful mind, too. He's got a sentimental side that you'll either find sappy or irresistible. Expect poems and flowers.

Libra Men: Sting, Michael Douglas, Usher, Matt Damon, Simon Cowell, Snoop Dogg, Eminem, Will Smith, John Lennon, Tommy Lee, Shaggy, Flea, Viggo Mortensen, Sean William Scott

THE SCORPIO MAN (October 23–November 21)

MYSTERY MAN | Intense! This smoldering, magnetic guy does nothing halfway. Although he doesn't let go of control easily, once he's in, he's in. Passionate and possessive, he needs a combo of security and spice. Relationships are about power for him. He loves a strong woman who also makes it safe for him to reveal his vulnerable side. The Scorpio man is extremely sensitive and doesn't trust easily. If you dump him, he'll obsess over you for years. Expect a few loyalty tests—and plenty of intrigue!

Scorpio Men: Ethan Hawke, P. Diddy, David Schwimmer, Bill Gates, Nick Lachey, Chris Noth, Prince Charles, Joaquin Phoenix, Ben Foster, Owen Wilson, Ryan Gosling

THE SAGITTARIUS MAN (November 22–December 21)

THE JOCKBOY JOKER | Sagittarius is the "bachelor sign," and while this guy can be loyal, he's eternally restless. He's a late bloomer and a lifelong class clown—all about adventure, inspiration and exploring the world. You're best off meeting him after he's sown his oats. The Sagittarius man needs a fellow adventurer, a best friend who keeps him in line and laughs at his jokes. Prissy types aren't his thing, but strong women with class and sass are always welcome!
Sagittarius Men: Brad Pitt, Jay–Z, Frank Sinatra, Jake Gyllenhal, Ben Stiller, Adam Brody, Samuel L. Jackson, Ozzy Osbourne, Jon Stewart, Frankie Muniz, Bruce Lee, Benjamin Bratt, Kiefer Sutherland, Steven Spielberg, Ed Harris

THE CAPRICORN MAN (December 22–January 19)

THE FAMILY GUY | Capricorn is the sign of loyalty and long–term commitments. He dates either for a fling or for a lifelong partner. He'll marry his high school sweetheart, or hold out for the woman with whom he can grow old. To make the cut, you must fit into his family and earn his parents' respect. He may seem boring, but still waters run deep. Underneath the calm exterior, he has a hidden naughty streak. Stick around and you'll find it!
Capricorn Men: Orlando Bloom, Nicholas Cage, Elvis Presley, Kid Rock, Jared Leto, Jude Law, Jim Carrey, Marilyn Manson, Eddie Vedder, R. Kelly, David Bowie, Ryan Seacrest, Ricky Martin, Denzel Washington, Martin Luther King Jr.

THE AQUARIUS MAN (January 20–February 18)

LET'S BE FRIENDS | He's a lighthearted, playful cutie who knows how to laugh at himself. No drama—this guy just wants to be your best friend. He loves practical jokes and entertains everyone with wacky impersonations. Don't expect grand displays of affection. Instead, let him show his love through friendship. The Aquarius guy will cheer you on through anything. Joining forces on a project that benefits society could bring you closer. It will also reveal his huge heart.
Aquarius Men: Justin Timberlake, John Travolta, Ashton Kutcher, Chris Rock, Wilmer Valderrama, Bobby Brown, Elijah Wood, Nick Carter, Burt Reynolds, James Dean, Bob Marley, Dr. Dre

THE PISCES MAN (February 19–March 20)

THE ARTIST | There's no mistaking this moody, broody guy who wears his emotions on his sleeve. He's Prince Charming and Mr. Sensitivity rolled into one. The Pisces man loves a tough, daring woman who says the things he's too shy to express. Since his sign rules guilt and compassion, he can't bear to hurt anyone. Make Pisces feel safe and he'll share his spicy fantasies. Although he may struggle to say how he really feels, this creative guy expresses his love through music, film, mix CDs, even poetry. Give him both solitude (when he's moody) and security (when he's needy), and he's yours.
Pisces Men: Freddie Prinze Jr., David Duchovny, Shaquille O'Neill, Bruce Willis, Kurt Cobain, Johnny Knoxville, Ja Rule, Bow Wow, Joel & Benji Madden, Adam Levine, Timbaland, Chris Martin, Billy Corgan, Johnny Cash

Wedding Planner

As the sign of tradition and public image, you want a big, impressive wedding, well–attended by childhood friends, family and important business associates. As with everything, you've probably worked long and hard to find a marriageable mate, so you might as well honor this accomplishment! Just because you're traditional doesn't mean you lack creative flair. Your solid good taste will ensure a classic wedding with added individual touches, like bongo drummers or a bonfire. Although you hide your sentimentality, inside you're an incurable romantic, so go old–fashioned with your special day. Hire the best photographer, splurge on a lavish buffet and treat everyone like a high–styling VIP. Capricorn Carolyn Bessette Kennedy proved the ultimate bride: her nuptials with JFK Jr. were shot in classic black–and–white film.

Bridezilla Alert: TRYING TO IMPRESS EVERYONE

Capricorns are perfectionists forever chasing goals, but there's a time to relax and live in the moment. Don't turn your wedding into an overambitious project; for example, buying a too–small dress that you're forced to diet into. If you let family and friends' opinions influence you too much, you'll forget that your wedding day is a unique expression of the love your created with your partner. A career–driven sign, you may feel obligated to invite your entire office. Remember, this is your wedding, not a networking event. Release your worries and include only the people you want there.

CAPRICORN

The Setting:

As the sign of the mountain goat, a rugged or wilderness landscape suits your earthy nature. You could marry at a ski lodge, or in a huge log cabin with a wood-burning fireplace and moose antlers on the wall. Alternatively, you might try a polo club, where you can wed in the high style many Capricorns love. Either way, you'll want to feel like the mistress of ceremonies, providing the best of everything for your guests. Opt for a rustic, hearty buffet with unusual dishes, like wild game hen or venison. You love crisp outdoor air, so plan a Fall or winter wedding, when you can light a fire and get cozy. Since you cherish time with your closest companions, you might rent an entire resort and put everyone up for the weekend.

The Dress:

Go classic and simple: Ralph Lauren, country chic or modern basic look best on you. For a twist, add a family heirloom, like your grandmother's wedding jewels or an intricate, handmade veil. Image is important to Capricorns, so your dress should be proper and parent–approved, but still glamorous. A high–necked gown, satin gloves, and other old–fashioned touches go far. Just don't let your concerns about what's "appropriate" steer you into frumpiness. Honor your inner bad girl with sexy lingerie and a frilly garter, kept hidden from all but your groom.

The Bridal Party:

You're ceremonious and nostalgic, so you'll probably have a large bridal party filled with siblings, favorite cousins and loyal childhood friends. Dress your brides-maids in simple satin gowns and muted colors like teal, forest green or dark red. Since you cherish history, you may incorporate family or cultural traditions into the ceremony. For example, the groomsmen could wear Scottish kilts and walk up the aisle to a bagpipe serenade.

{Suit yourself}

Stylin'

Colors: Beige, gray, forest green
Focus areas: Knees, skin, teeth
Fabric: Flannel
Best Looks: Hiking boots, cashmere or cableknit sweaters, leather gloves, antique jewelry, pin–striped blazers, button–down shirts, leather jackets
Stay Away From: Anything tight, synthetic fibers, trendy cuts, overstyled hair, loud colors, athletic gear, low–cut shirts

14

Keep it simple, sister. You're the fresh, all–American girl who looks best in basics. Capricorns Kate Moss and Christy Turlington exemplify the minimalism that suits your sign. You're right at home in muted colors, fisherman sweaters, a leather jacket and jeans in a classic cut. As the sign of the mountain goat, you need well–made shoes or even hiking boots. Capricorn rules the lower legs, so show yours off in knee boots.

Capricorn is the sign of the executive, so invest in at least one power suit. You look great in a pinstriped blazer and man–tailored shirts. You can even wear ties or menswear, like Capricorns Diane Keaton and Ellen DeGeneres. You should also have a couple evening gowns for VIP events.

Resist the temptation to dress racy, like Capricorn Dolly Parton—even if you've got the assets to fill out a low–cut dress. Aim for a fresh, down–to–earth look. On weekdays, opt for natural makeup and conservative touches. When you're not at the office, throw your hair in a ponytail and relax like the stylish earth girl you are.

your celebrity starmates

Ellen DeGeneres
Christy Turlington
Kate Moss
Mary J. Blige
Julia Louis–Dreyfuss
Diane Keaton
Sienna Miller
Kate Bosworth
Amanda Peete
Estella Warren
Dolly Parton
Sade
Annie Lennox
Dido
Mia Tyler
Eartha Kitt
Donna Summer
Eliza Dushku
Aaliyah
Tia Carrere

Fitness & Well-Being

Body Part:
Knees, teeth, skin, bones

Health & Fitness Style:
You have the persistence to go the distance. Cross–country running, hiking, mountain biking, marathons, competitive soccer or rugby appeal to you. A workaholic, you'll have to make extra effort to maintain your physical fitness. Think of it as a long-term professional investment that will help you produce better results. Because Capricorns like achievements, try competitive team sports, especially ones with medals and trophies. You rule the bones and knees, so beware getting yours out of alignment. A steady sign, you make a great surfer, like Capricorn Kate Bosworth.

Keeping That Glow:
Massages and bodywork are great for you, as you hold the weight of the world on your shoulders. You worry like no other sign and can literally make yourself sick. Any illness you suffer is probably stress–induced, or a result of holding too much inside. Long walks, jogging or competitive sports will help you release tension. Balancing work and rest is key. Capricorns can sleep for hours, so schedule and all–day snooze marathon at least once a month. Connecting to the earth, your ruling element, grounds you. A motorcycle or scooter ride Zens you out, as does a long ride in a convertible sports car. Or, hop on a mountain bike and explore some rugged terrain.

Food & Eating Habits:
Capricorns do best on a schedule, so think structure: be sure to eat enough and eat regularly. Don't start working before you eat a balanced breakfast—you'll need fuel for the long day ahead. Capricorns are adventurous, eclectic eaters and your tastes can swing from traditional family recipes to fine dining. You love hearty food or anything that will keep fuel in your tank for a long time. Avoid empty calories or fast food so you don't have to fill up every hour. As an earth sign, you'll do well with organic or farm–fresh food. Stock up on locally–grown produce from the farmer's market or join a neighborhood food co–op.

family

You're extremely loyal to your family and can be quite traditional at heart. Your natural strength and stability causes family to lean on as their rock. In many ways, you love this role. You're a strong provider and you're at your best in a crisis. It's tough for you to show that you're struggling, and only your family sees your sensitive side. Capricorns from unhappy or unstable homes can suffer for years. You may isolate yourself from relatives, even growing bitter and distrustful. Work on forgiving your family's shortcomings, and lean on your lifelong friends as an extended family.

Issue to Manage: Being too attached to your family

Family loyalty is beautiful, but there's a time to break away. If you come from a stable home, your parents may be your best friends. If you come from a tougher environment, you may resent your parents, blaming your unhappiness on their mistakes. There's a time to cut the cord and forge your own identity. Don't let your irrational fears stop you from discovering who you are.

The Capricorn Parent:
+You hold it together through thick and thin, providing what your children need.
−Your difficulty showing emotion can make your children long for a more nurturing touch.

The Capricorn Child:
+You're serious, disciplined and follow the rules.
−You're an old soul—go out and play with the other kids!

The Capricorn Sibling:
+You're loyal and protective, sticking up for your sibs even at your own expense.
−You resent your siblings for having all the fun while you play the good–girl role.

friendship

Best Friends:
Taurus, Cancer, Virgo, Pisces
Choppy Waters:
Aries, Gemini, Libra, Sagittarius

Capricorn is the sign of the class president, and you may become quite popular without even trying. At the end of the day though, you trust only a few close friends. Capricorns are highly nostalgic and make friends for life. You want to tell your grandchildren, "We've been best friends for 80 years!" You're only interested in things of quality that are built to last, and that also goes for friendship.

Your have two types of friends: the tight circle of your personal pals, and your "professional friendships" that you establish for networking purposes. You're ambitious enough to keep your contacts fresh. Because you're cautious around those you don't know, you treat casual acquaintances with polite reserve. Only close friends will see your dark, moody side—and the quirky humor you keep under wraps, too.

Capricorns can be pessimistic, worrying about every little detail. Although you keep that million-dollar smile shining for everyone else, when alone, you easily slip into doom and gloom. Sometimes, you need to vent your stress rather than shut the world out as you obsess over worst-case scenarios. You think you must maintain a "public face" and a "private face," not letting others know you're struggling until you've finally figured out what's eating you. But this only leaves you stuck longer, sinking into unnecessary depression. Make sure you pour your worries out to a few close friends who will comfort and reassure you.

home décor

Capricorns love antiques. Your place could look like an overdone flea market or, if you're a modern Cap girl, you may go minimalist, using muted colors, steel furniture and sparse decor. Just try not to make your home look like an electronics showroom or an antique roadshow gone awry. Aim for a nice blend of heart and soul, classic and modern, comfortable and utilitarian, pre-fab and handmade, and you'll strike an attractive balance.

A great work area is vital for you, so invest in a heavy executive-style desk made of solid wood and a supportive leather chair. Add VIP flourishes like a gold pen and inkwell, a monogrammed letter opener, even an engraved nameplate. If you're a workaholic, hire a decorator or enlist a stylish friend, because it could take forever for you to find basic furniture. Worse, you might buy everything in one shot, regretting half the purchases when they arrive. Remember, decorating is a form of self-expression, not just a practical necessity, so take time to do it right. You need a homey, cozy space to return to after a hard day's work because you get depressed easily otherwise.

Capricorns like reliable and long-lasting items of quality—especially all-American or name brand items, and you'll splurge on a few. In the bedroom, go for Ralph Lauren flannel sheets, and a plaid or corduroy duvet by Tommy Hilfiger in navy, burgundy, forest green or gray. Don't go overboard on the dark colors, though—add life with fresh flowers or a few bright pieces of art. Capricorns rule the lower legs, so chances are you have a nice collection of boots and sexy heels. An organized closet is essential to keep your cherished garments looking like new.

You're nostalgic, so incorporate family pieces, memorabilia and framed photos. As the sign of achievement, you should display awards, trophies or anything that honors your accomplishments. You can be a bit obsessive-compulsive about having things just so, and may not invite guests over as a result. However, if you're too isolated, you grow melancholy. Temper this by creating a cozy living room that serves as a "play area" for your cherished family and friends.

Party Planner

Party? What's that? Capricorn is a workaholic by nature, and you can even be a bit of a hermit. Most of the time, you're driving yourself toward a goal, and can't be bothered to pause for something as "impractical" as a party. You probably have a small crew of lifelong friends that you hang with on a regular basis. Your social needs are simple, and you're content to have people drop by for a card game, a round of Trivial Pursuit or a cup of herbal tea.

As the zodiac's career sign, you'll opt for parties with a networking component. Bring lots of business cards and wear your sharpest blazer. You're always ripe to exchange numbers with someone who can further your goals—and you never know whom you'll meet!

That said, you're the VIP sign, so when you do throw a bash, you like to display your status with a grandiose affair. A traditionalist at heart, you love the major holidays. With the office closed, you have no excuse not to relax! Capricorn is a family–oriented sign, so include your clan in your party plans. Get a dining room table with extending leaves and serve a large, multi–course dinner. Or take everyone out to your favorite family–style restaurant. You love history, so a historically–themed party could stoke your fires. Many Capricorns also have a hidden wild streak, and parties are a great time to express it.

Bottom line, if you're throwing a party, you want to do it right. You can be quite self–critical and worrisome, and although you mask your insecurities well, you want everyone to think highly of you. You're the sign of public image, after all, and you guard your reputation closely. Just remember, you only live once. What good are all those accomplishments if you don't celebrate them?

career

Capricorn rules the zodiac's career sector, so you're in your element at work. You're driven, willing to work long and hard, and often become the backbone of the office. You're a loyal "company woman," willing to do the dirty work if it will ultimately get you ahead. Some Caps might even step on a person or two to climb the success ladder, so be careful not to become ruthless in your quest. You must have a job you're proud of, because you identify strongly with your position and take great pride in it. The sign of leadership, you make a great manager who insists on high standards. Your dream is a cushy corner office at a well-established company with security and benefits so you can provide for your family.

Pitfalls:

Strictness: Capricorns like rules, but you can be too intense about enforcing them. This will stifle or alienate people, causing them to rebel. Ruling with an iron fist will collapse the great teams you build. Think of yourself as a mentor and lead with humanity instead.

Sacrificing your personal life: It's great to have a career, but unless you're a doctor, you're not on call 24/7. A work–life balance is essential for your long–term health. Go ahead, shut down that computer and head home. It will save you bitterness and burnout.

Best careers for Capricorn:

manager
architect
financial planner
CEO
public speaker
investment banker
graphic designer
technical illustrator
doctor
real estate developer
school principal
attorney
creative director

20

money

Your Money Management Style:

Capricorns have a natural financial acumen. That doesn't mean you always have money—you're usually willing to risk short–term sacrifices for the big–picture payoff. Your sign rules structure, so you like budgets and do everything with an eye to the future. You're careful, economical, ambitious, hard–working and a natural provider. Be careful not to foster co–dependence with family and friends, though, or you could become a prisoner of your paycheck.

Your Spending Habits:

Capricorn rules the zodiac's career house and you have an investment mindset. You excel at long–term planning. In the short run, that means you can be tight with your cash, preferring to save it for a rainy day and missing all the fun! You're very concerned with your status and career, so you'll splurge to make a good impression: business cards on heavy stock, tailored suits, meals at the "right" restaurants. Be careful not to drain your wallet on your appearance.

What You Buy:
Power suits, leather shoes and accessories, school and office supplies, expensive meals at large VIP restaurants, dinner for people you want to impress, gifts and essentials for your family, lots of black and gray clothes

How to Attract More Money: Loosen up!
Budgets and rules are great, but hello—sometimes you need to let loose! For your worrisome sign, it's important to experience being a little extravagant and seeing that everything will actually turn out fine. You may save and save, holding on so tightly to your money that you lose perspective. Releasing your grip will usher in fresh new sources of flow, and prevent you from turning into Madame Scrooge. Indulge in the occasional impulse buy or impractical purchase and you'll be much happier.

Travel

You're an earth sign and you crave fresh outdoor air. While you'll be tempted to bring your work with you on vacation, don't do it! You may have a few irrational fears about taking off for a trip—maybe because you're unsure you've earned the right—but leave those at home with your laptop. The only distraction you need is a stunning landscape or a good book to read poolside at a luxury resort. Worrying is a Capricorn trademark and you may even be afraid to fly by airplane, or to contract germs in a big city. Challenge those neuroses head–on and go for it. Once you awaken your adventurous spirit, you'll be a travel addict!

As soon as you slip into lounge mode, you'll wonder what took you so long. You make an awesome traveler once you get past your initial reservations. The earthier among you might slip on a backpack and a good pair of hiking boots, and hit the camping trails for adventure. You may even try an extreme outdoor sport like rock climbing or white–water rafting. As the sign of the mountain goat, you're sure–footed enough to handle rugged terrain. For other Caps, that "terrain" might be the manicured streets of a European city or a five–star resort stocked with complimentary towels. Whatever you prefer, vacation provides you with the opportunity to practice the art of receiving for a change. Rather than giving and giving, it's now your turn to abandon your selflessness and be taken care of—the way only a seasoned world traveler can!

january	start something new
february	money!
march	communicate!
april	family
may	flirting
june	get in shape!
july	relationships
august	get married
september	vacation
october	career & achievement
november	friends & networking
december	finish everything!

Your Yearlong Planetary Planner

january | it's all about you!

Make a fresh start! As the Sun enters your sign, you kick off your personal New Year. Think new! This is the time to launch projects, debut a new image, and take on a leading role. It's all about you now. Don't let demanding types take away from your "me" time. Say yes only to offers that take your dreams to the next level. Express yourself in a big way—be bold and fearless. You have the stage and the world is listening!

february | money & makeovers

Last month was all about getting in touch with the person you've become. Now, it's time to build an environment—and an income—that reflect the new you. Treat yourself to a makeover. Stock your fridge with gourmet groceries. Add a few fabulous pieces to your wardrobe, or pick up a beautiful vase or bed cover. Money is highlighted now. Are you earning what you're worth? Is it time for a new job or a raise? Does your budget allow you to both splurge and save for your dreams? A financial advisor or smart money manager can help now.

march | communicate!

Communication is this month's theme. If you haven't expressed what's on your mind, do it now! Send off emails, return calls, write letters, reach out to old friends. It's a great month for writers, too. Your mind bubbles with ideas, so jot them down in a notebook. This month rules siblings and friends, so make time to connect with yours. Short trips and your neighborhood are also featured. Organize a block party. Explore your favorite local haunts or discover new ones. Grab a pal for a bike ride or power-walk, and enjoy an inspiring talk.

april | family matters

Home and family are where it's at now. Cozy up your household—add fluffy towels, scented soaps, soft sheets and fresh flowers. Don't overdo on parties. Instead, opt for home-cooked meals, a good book and your favorite DVD. Your energy is low-key now, so book some private time. Spend quality time with your parents and cherished family members, or send them a thoughtful card. Female energy and femininity are strong now. Surround yourself with comforting, inspiring women. Get in touch with the powerful woman that you are.

may | romance & fun

Fun, fun, fun! Your energy turns light and playful now. The planets favor romance, and creativity this month. If you're single, this is your month to get out and flirt! If you're in a relationship, bring the magic back with lighthearted dates. Grab your sweetie and head to a fiesta. Dive into a creative project, and let your inner artist emerge. Children are highlighted. If you want to get pregnant, the stars are on your side. Spending time with young people can restore your own childlike wonder.

june | get fit & organized!

After an indulgent month, it's time to get organized. The planets morph you from party girl into the Queen of Clean. Sort out your calendar, projects and workspace. Attack the clutter and get your life back on track. This month's energy also sends you on a health kick. Hit the gym, walk around the neighborhood, buy a yoga or Pilates DVD. Pick up some fresh, organic groceries and prepare a healthy meal. Bring your eating and life back into balance. (For great tips, see the Fitness section!)

july | relationships get serious

Happy half-birthday! You're midway through your astrological year now, and the planets shift your focus to relationships and other people. Committed partnerships, both personal and professional, are highlighted. If you've longed to get serious with that special someone, now is a great time. If you and a close person have been having trouble understanding each other's perspectives, you may finally see the light. Contract signings go well. If you're getting married, this is the month to say "I do!"

august | it's in the details

How deep are your bonds with people? You'll find out this month, as the planets bring out your most intimate side. You feel passionate, driven, even mystical— your life could feel like a spicy novel! At times, you or someone around you may seem a bit secretive. Solve the mystery. The stars also focus on joint resources and large amounts of money. Real estate, income taxes, investments, inheritances, and credit cards are all highlighted. Pay off debts, write a living will, invest in property. Research everything thoroughly, as your mind is sharp. Pay attention to every detail!

september | vacation & inspiration

After an intense month, you're ready for a vacation! The stars light up your sector of long-distance travel now, beckoning you to pack your bags and head for distant shores. Book a getaway outside city limits, even if it's just a long weekend. If you can't leave town, expand your horizons by attending an inspiring class, lecture or workshop. Higher education is featured now, so apply to schools or for scholarships. Step outside your comfort zone at every opportunity. Explore another culture. Avoid petty squabbles. Enjoy soul-searching conversations.

october | career & fame

Career, achievement and ambition are all featured now. Keep your eye on your goals and aim for them! People relate to you as a natural leader now, so take charge and step boldly into what you want. If you haven't commanded the respect you deserve, ask for it. If you're looking for fame, this is the month to put yourself directly in the spotlight. You could be honored and noticed for all your hard work. Acknowledge yourself for how far you've come!

november | friends & networking

There's strength in numbers, and the planets urge you to team up now. What better way to get your message out there than with a fun and lively crew? If career is your passion, join a networking group or attend a professional group meeting. If you're looking to expand your circle of friends, try a book club, co-ed singles group, or an intramural sports team. Reconnect with old friends by hosting a party or reunion. Humanitarian efforts are also featured this month, so volunteer for a worthy cause. Get out and mingle!

december | handle your business

Yawn! The Sun completes the last leg of its journey around your zodiac wheel, making you a little sleepy. Hold off on anything new and instead, think completion. Finish any lingering loose ends. You'll want a clean slate next month, when your personal New Year begins! Return phone calls, donate old clothes to charity, and resolve any conflicts. Get plenty of rest, and pour out your feelings in a journal or creative work. Your dreams are full of vivid messages, and your healing powers are strong. Consider volunteering at a hospital or with the elderly.